GERALD R. Ford

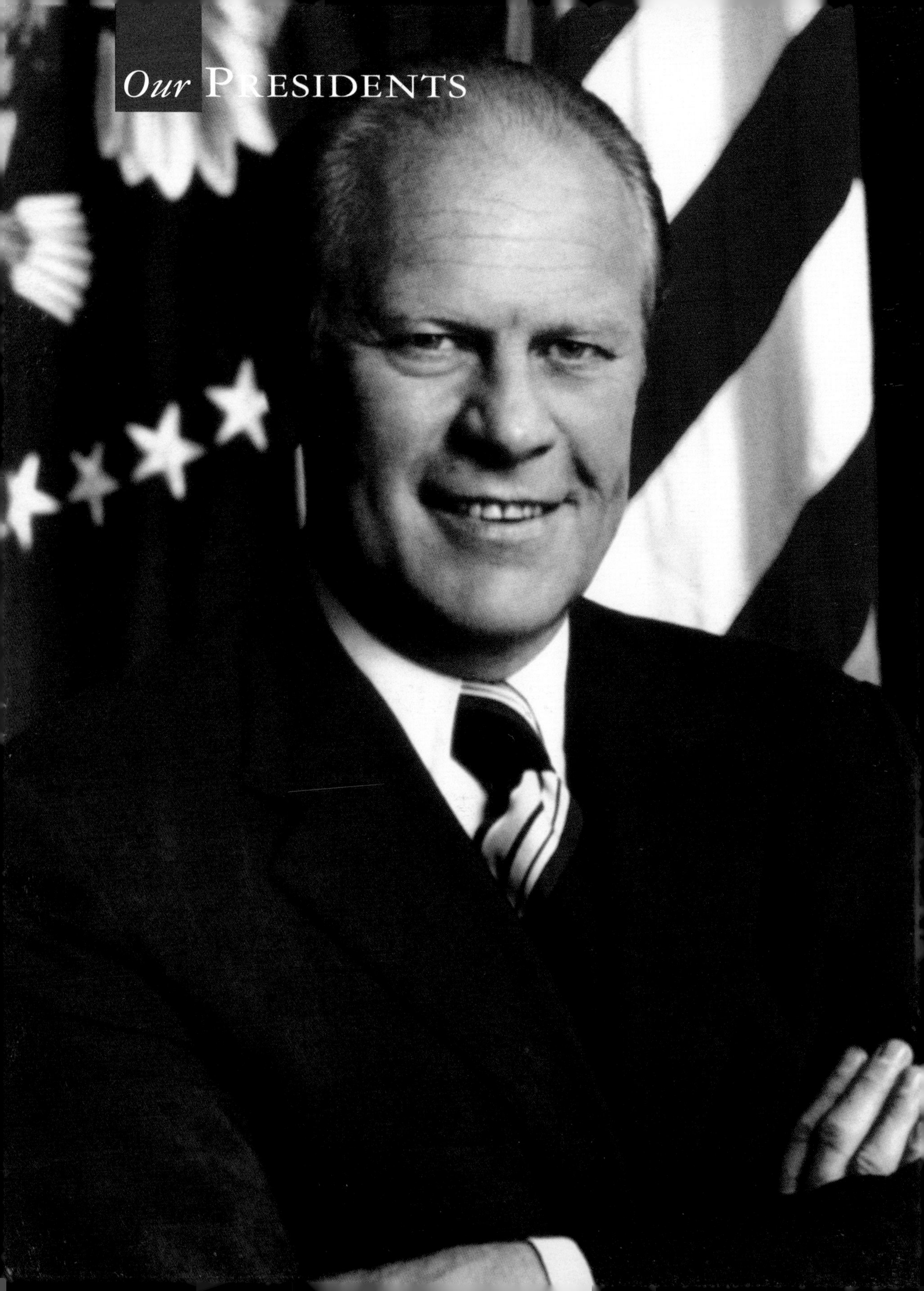

Gerald R. Ford

Our Thirty-Eighth President

By Sandra Francis

SPIRIT
of America®

The Child's World®
Chanhassen, Minnesota

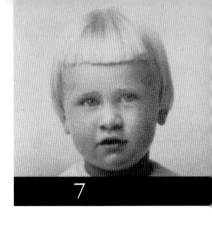

7

GERALD R. *Ford*

Published in the United States of America by The Child's World®
PO Box 326 • Chanhassen, MN 55317-0326 • 800-599-READ • www.childsworld.com

Acknowledgments
The Creative Spark: Mary Francis-DeMarois, Project Director; Elizabeth Sirimarco Budd, Series Editor;
Robert Court, Design and Art Direction; Janine Graham, Page Layout; Jennifer Moyers, Production

The Child's World®: Mary Berendes, Publishing Director; Red Line Editorial, Fact Research;
Cindy Klingel, Curriculum Advisor; Robert Noyed, Historical Advisor

Photos
All photos are courtesy of the Gerald R. Ford Library, Ann Arbor, Michigan.

Registration
The Child's World®, Spirit of America®, and their associated logos are the sole property and
registered trademarks of The Child's World®.

Library of Congress Cataloging-in-Publication Data
Francis, Sandra.
    Gerald R. Ford : our thirty-eighth president / by Sandra Francis.
        p. cm.
    Includes bibliographical references and index.
    ISBN 1-56766-872-0 (lib. bdg. : alk. paper)
    1. Ford, Gerald R., 1913– —Juvenile literature. 2. Presidents—United States—Biography—Juvenile
literature. [1. Ford, Gerald R., 1913– 2. Presidents.] I. Title.
    E866 .F7 2001
    973.925'092—dc21

                                                00-011489

12   29   31

Contents

Chapter ONE	*Happy Childhood*	6
Chapter TWO	*Aboard the USS* Monterey	14
Chapter THREE	*A Strong Start*	22
Chapter FOUR	*The Presidency*	30
	Time Line	38
	Glossary Terms	40
	Our Presidents	42
	Presidential Facts	46
	For Further Information	47
	Index	48

Happy Childhood

Gerald R. Ford was born on July 14, 1913. He is shown here with his mother, Dorothy.

GERALD R. FORD JR. WAS NOT ELECTED THE 38th president of the United States. Instead, he was a vice president who took over the presidency at a very difficult time in history. President Richard Nixon had been accused of illegal activities. He denied any wrongdoing for two years. But it became clear that the nation's leader had been dishonest. In the summer of 1974, the stunned American people watched as Nixon resigned from office, which means he gave up his position. Americans had lost faith in the presidency and in their government. Against this backdrop, Nixon's vice president, Gerald Ford, took the oath of office on August 9, 1974.

As Ford entered office, he told Americans that "the long national nightmare" was over.

Right away, he wanted to prove that he was very different from President Nixon. He wanted the nation to see that a decent leader was once again in the White House. Ford may have been the perfect person to enter office at that time. He had long been a member of Congress and was known as an honest, hardworking man. He was someone people could trust. Gerald Ford often said that his best personal qualities came from his childhood in the Midwest.

Ford has said he was very lucky to have a strong, happy family during his childhood.

Although Ford's childhood was a happy one, it did have an unusual beginning. He was born in Omaha, Nebraska, on July 14, 1913. His parents were Leslie Lynch King and Dorothy Gardner King. They named their new son Leslie Lynch King Jr. From the start of the marriage, Mr. King had been an unkind husband. Two weeks after little Leslie's birth, Dorothy and her son left

7

▶ Even though Jerry Ford could write better with his left hand, his teachers and parents tried to force him to use his right hand, which was then a common practice. About the time he was learning to write, Ford developed a stutter in his speech. Finally, his teachers let him write with his left hand, and the stuttering stopped. From then on, Ford was right-handed when standing and left-handed when sitting.

▶ Jerry was voted the most popular senior at his high school.

home. They went to live with her parents in Grand Rapids, Michigan. Soon Dorothy and Leslie King were divorced, and she had full care of her beautiful, blond-haired baby boy.

Dorothy and "Junie," as she called her son, enjoyed a happy new beginning. One day at a church social, Dorothy met a wonderful man named Gerald R. Ford. He was nice to her and to Junie. He was successful and owned his own paint business. After a year of dating, Gerald and Dorothy married on February 1, 1916.

Gerald loved Junie as if he were his own child. As Junie grew up, his family began to call him Jerry and then Gerald R. Ford Jr. (Many years later, in 1935, he officially changed his name.) Over the years, the Ford's had three more sons, Thomas, Richard, and James. The Fords were a close, happy family. In fact, until he was a teenager, Jerry did not know that Gerald R. Ford Sr. was not his real father.

Jerry's years at South High School in Grand Rapids were busy ones. He was not only an excellent student, but a popular athlete as well. Good grades earned him membership in the school's honor society. Although Jerry dreamed of becoming a famous baseball player,

8

he was even better at football. His skill on the playing field earned him spots on the All-City and All-State football teams. After practice and on weekends, Jerry earned spending money working at the family business. He also worked at a local restaurant.

When Jerry was ready to enter college, the family did not have enough money to pay for it. The Great Depression had brought hard times to the country and to the Ford family.

Jerry Ford (far left) was very active during his high school years. One thing he enjoyed was scouting. At age 14, he achieved the rank of Eagle Scout. In the summer of 1929, he and his troop served as guides at a scout camp. There he discovered that he liked meeting people and being a leader.

Jerry (second from left) posed for this photograph with his stepfather and half-brothers on the front steps of their home.

The Depression was a period in U.S. history when there was little business activity. Many people could not find work. In these rough times, Jerry's good grades and athletic ability paid off. The principal of his high school arranged for Jerry to receive a scholarship, an award that would help pay for school. Jerry later said that this "was the luckiest break I ever had." In 1931, he enrolled at the University of Michigan at Ann Arbor.

10

Over the next four years, Jerry earned good grades. He was also a football star and played on the school's national championship teams in 1932 and 1933. He was voted the most valuable player in 1934. Jerry still needed to earn extra money, however. While at the university, he took several jobs to help pay his expenses. All this hard work paid off. It led the way to many rewards, both in college and in his future. In June of 1935, Jerry graduated from the University of Michigan.

One of Jerry's next goals was to study law at Yale University, one of the nation's best schools. Money for education was still difficult to come by, and he knew he would have to continue working. He found a job coaching football and boxing at Yale and hoped this would earn enough money to pay for school. But it wasn't easy. At first, Yale Law School did not accept him. Many people wanted to attend Yale. The school only accepted one out of every four students who applied, usually those with the highest grades. Jerry's grades were good, but they weren't the very best. In addition, Jerry was working full-time as a coach. The Yale

Jerry is shown here in 1933, during football practice at the University of Michigan. After graduating, he received offers to play for two professional football teams: the Detroit Lions and the Green Bay Packers. Jerry turned the offers down. His dream was to become a lawyer.

professors thought he would be too busy with his job to work hard at his studies.

Jerry didn't give up. In the summer of 1937, he took more courses at the University of Michigan. The following spring, he presented Yale with his good grades. Jerry had earned his way into one of the best schools in the country! He completed his law degree in 1941. Even though he still worked full-time as a coach, he graduated in the top 25 percent of his class.

Jerry returned to Michigan to set up a law practice in Grand Rapids. His partner was a college friend, Philip A. Buchen. As always,

Jerry kept very busy. He taught a course in business law at the University of Grand Rapids and coached the school's football team. He also became active in the Republican Party, one of the nation's two most powerful **political parties.**

But about six months later, on December 7, 1941, Gerald Ford's career was interrupted. While driving home from his office, he heard very bad news. Japanese warplanes had attacked the U.S. naval base in Pearl Harbor, Hawaii. This violent act forced the United States to enter World War II, and the nation would need its young men to go to battle.

Interesting Facts

▶ The Japanese attack on Pearl Harbor on December 7, 1941, killed more than 2,400 Americans, sunk or damaged 18 U.S. ships, and destroyed or damaged more than 200 U.S. airplanes.

Jerry (right) and his fellow football coaches are shown preparing for practice at Yale University in 1935. Jerry accepted the coaching job hoping that he would one day attend Yale Law School. His dream came true in 1938.

Chapter Two

Aboard the USS Monterey

At the start of World War II, the U.S. military needed young men to fight for the country. Ford joined the U.S. Navy in 1942.

IN APRIL OF 1942, FORD JOINED THE U.S. NAVY. He completed his basic training and was quickly **promoted** from ensign to lieutenant. Ford's first assignment was as the athletic training **officer** at the preflight school in North Carolina. His job was to coach the navy's future pilots in sports, which kept them in top physical condition. Although this assignment was not what Ford wanted, he did his best. His commanding officer said Ford was "an outstanding officer, one of the finest in the station, and an excellent shipmate."

Finally, in the summer of 1943, the navy assigned Ford to sea duty on the USS *Monterey*. The *Monterey* was an aircraft carrier that had been rebuilt for combat. It could carry more than 1,500 sailors and 45 bomber and fighter aircraft.

14

In October, the *Monterey* was ready to go into battle. It joined Admiral Halsey's Third Fleet in the South Pacific. The crew of the *Monterey* first saw action on November 19, 1943, when its planes fired on a Japanese base in the Gilbert Islands. The battle lasted for three weeks. Ford's job was to stand at the back of the ship and tell soldiers when and where to fire their guns. He later remembered that his battle experiences were terrifying. "The Japanese planes came after us with a vengeance," he said.

In the spring of 1943, Ford began service on an aircraft carrier, the USS Monterey *(above), in the South Pacific. The ship's crew took part in many of the major battles in the Pacific during World War II.*

Ford made friends with Captain Hundt, a great football fan. This friendship soon led to Ford's new position as the assistant navigator, although he had no training in **navigation.** But with the teaching of Commander Pappy Atwood, Ford learned the job quickly. He liked his new position. He was in the middle of the action, where navy leaders made important decisions.

Beginning in January of 1944, the *Monterey* and its crew were in many major battles. They attacked enemy ships and shores. Japanese pilots came after all the U.S. aircraft carriers and cruisers in the region. One day, a torpedo meant for the *Monterey* narrowly missed it. The *Monterey* fought off its Japanese attackers for 24 hours straight. The mangled U.S. cruisers sailed away from the battle, but the *Monterey* was still going strong. It attacked its enemy one more time, allowing the cruisers to escape. In just a little over a year, the *Monterey* and its crew of brave men earned 10 battle stars (special honors).

Surviving all that the enemy could throw at the *Monterey* was just the beginning. In December of 1944, the crew faced something that became even more dangerous than enemy fire. "The Great Typhoon" was one of the worst storms ever seen in the Pacific Ocean. Commander Atwood issued an immediate order to tie the planes tightly to the deck. The crew of the *Monterey* could see other ships being tossed around like toys, then sinking into the furious ocean. Picking up survivors was almost impossible, and many lives were lost to the storm.

Lieutenant Ford awoke to the smell of smoke. Grabbing his helmet, he tried to reach his battle station. "As I stepped on the flight deck, the ship suddenly rolled about 25 degrees. I lost my footing, fell to the deck flat on my face, and started sliding toward the port [left] side as if I were on a toboggan slide," he later recalled.

Ford slid, feet first, 109 feet across the flight deck. As his body rushed toward the sea, he spotted a rim of metal that went around the deck. "I put out my feet and hit it," Ford later remembered.

Ford is shown here (seated second from right) with other gunnery officers aboard the Monterey. *Their job was to tell soldiers when and where to fire their guns.*

17

"Instead of going over the side, I twisted my body as my feet hit the rim, and I landed in the narrow catwalk just below the port edge of the flight deck."

The water rushed by him only two feet away. Ford clung to the rim until he caught his breath. He managed to pull himself back up and ran to his battle station. What he saw was disaster. Airplanes had been torn loose, and fires were spreading from the front to the back of the ship. "The planes bounded around the hangar deck like trapped and terrified birds," he said. "Showers of sparks flew as the planes crashed into each other and against the sides of the ship."

Working feverishly, the crew pushed torpedoes, bombs, and other explosives overboard. Only one of the ship's engines was working, and it couldn't carry all this weight. There was little water pressure in the hoses, so fighting the fires was difficult. Struggling bravely, the crew battled the raging sea to keep the *Monterey* upright.

A radio message from Admiral Halsey ordered them to abandon ship. Nearby cruisers were waiting to rescue the crew.

Interesting Facts

▸ As "The Great Typhoon" raged, the winds were reported to be about 124 miles per hour. Waves reached heights of nearly 100 feet.

Commander Atwood refused to abandon the ship. He asked Halsey for more time to save the *Monterey*. For another 40 minutes, Atwood and the brave crew struggled to get the ship upright in the fierce wind. This reduced the ship's motion so the crew could put out the fires without dodging the airplanes. Atwood's plan to save the ship and his men was successful. Seven hours later, the *Monterey* found its way to a safe harbor in the western Caroline Islands. When it was all over, three men had died, and 40 more were injured. The navy determined that the ship was unfit for further service. It was taken out of the water for major repairs.

Even after this frightening experience, Ford still wanted to be assigned to sea duty. Instead, he was ordered back to the United States and promoted. Ford's service report stated, "He is

Ford and his friend Truman Walling were photographed on the flight deck of the Monterey *in 1944. Although the ship's crew faced many dangerous battles with the enemy, the worst event of all was the typhoon that struck in December of 1944. Ford almost lost his life in the violent storm.*

▸ Ford remained in the U.S. Naval Reserves until 1963. This meant that in the event of a war, he could have been recalled to serve.

▸ Ford is a member of the American Legion, Veterans of Foreign Wars, and AMVETS, which are all organizations for people who served in the U.S. military.

steady, reliable, and resourceful…. His unfailing good humor, pleasing personality, and natural ability as a leader made him well liked and respected by the officers and men." These qualities had always been typical of Ford, and they would continue to be throughout his life.

Ford was assigned to the U.S. Navy Training Command in Glenview, Illinois. He was to train new officers for duty at sea and in the air. Ford wished to enter into combat again and applied for a position on a ship called the *Coral Sea*. But Japan surrendered on August 14, 1945. World War II was over, and Ford was discharged from the navy the following February.

Ford built a basketball court on the hangar deck of the Monterey, *knowing that exercise would keep the men in good condition.*

BEFORE WORLD WAR II, the United States rarely became involved with the affairs of other countries. Americans preferred to stay out of problems around the world, which is a policy known as **isolationism.** But then Germany's **Nazi Party,** led by Adolf Hitler, came to power in the early 1930s. Soon it threatened to overtake all of Europe.

At the same time, Japan was aggressively attacking other Asian nations. On December 7, 1941, the Japanese bombed Pearl Harbor (above), the U.S. naval base in Hawaii. This act killed 2,403 Americans and wounded more than 1,000. The next day, the United States declared war. It could no longer remain isolated, separate from other countries. To protect its people and its shores, the U.S. went to war.

World War II changed Gerald Ford's view of the world, as well as the views of other Americans. "Before the war I was a typical Midwest isolationist," he once said. "I returned understanding we could never be isolated again. We were and are one world. It was clear to me, it was inevitable to me, that this country was obligated to lead in this new world. We had won the war. It was up to us to keep the peace."

Chapter THREE

A Strong Start

Ford returned to Michigan in 1946 and took a job at a law firm in Grand Rapids. He was very active in the community and became well known.

GERALD FORD RETURNED TO GRAND RAPIDS after four years of military duty. A position with one of the best law firms in town was waiting for him. Julius Amberg, a senior partner at the firm, took Ford under his wing. He taught him how to be the best business lawyer he could be. Ford did not disappoint his employers. He was the first one to arrive at work in the morning and the last one to leave at night.

Ford became known for his honesty and hard work. This linked him to many important people, who would help him succeed. Although he considered himself lucky, Ford also had faith in his abilities. He was willing to work hard and had a natural gift for earning the trust of powerful people.

In 1948, Ford decided to run for the U.S. House of Representatives, which is part of Congress. To win the position, he had to challenge Bartel J. Jonkman, who had been in the House for 10 years. Like Ford, Jonkman was a Republican. To enter the election, Ford had to win the **nomination** of the Republican Party.

Ford asked John Stiles, a former classmate and writer, to be his **campaign** manager. Neither Ford nor Stiles had any experience in politics, the work of the government. But together they created a plan to put Ford into office.

In 1948, Ford decided to enter politics. He entered the race for a seat in the House of Representatives.

23

Ford did not tell anyone he planned to be a **candidate** until the last minute. That way, Jonkman and his supporters would not have much time to campaign against him. The plan worked, and the Republicans chose Ford as their candidate. He then went on to win the election on November 2, 1948, with 61 percent of the vote. Ford took his seat in the House of Representatives the following January.

It was during Ford's first days in Congress that he met Richard Nixon, a well-known representative from California. Nixon approached Ford with a handshake, congratulating him on his big win in the election. Ford was surprised that Nixon—or anyone—had heard of him. Nixon became a longtime friend, as well as an important step in Ford's path to the presidency.

From the start, Ford promised himself that he would not allow other Republicans to pressure him into making decisions. Instead, he wanted to make decisions for himself. His friendly personality and firm beliefs allowed him to disagree with others without making enemies. These qualities made him a successful **politician.** In fact, Ford spent the next 25 years in the House of Representatives.

▶ Before the election of 1948, Ford made a campaign promise. He said that if he won the election, he would work at a dairy farm for two weeks. He kept his promise: "There I was, every morning … helping with the cows, cleaning up the barn, you name it."

Ford's stepfather (far right) used to say, "The harder you work, the better your luck." These words guided Gerald R. Ford Jr. as he entered the world of politics. He is shown here with his parents after winning the Republican nomination in 1948.

He was so respected in this position that the people of Michigan reelected him 12 times. In every election, he always won more than 60 percent of the vote.

During his years in the House, Ford held many important positions. In 1951, he became a member of the House Appropriations Committee. This committee makes decisions about how the government should raise and spend money. In 1961, he became a member of the Defense Appropriations Subcommittee. This committee determines how the military should spend its money. Many people encouraged Ford to run for the Senate or to try to become the governor of Michigan. He always refused. His goal was to become the Speaker of the House, the head of the House of Representatives.

In 1965, Ford was elected to the position of minority leader of the House of Representatives. In this post, he represented the Republicans in the House. (The Republicans were the minority because they had fewer members than the Democrats at the time.) Ford held the position for eight years. As minority leader, he traveled around the country and gave more than 200 speeches each year. He became well known. Through-out his time in Congress, Ford always had good relations with other politicians, even those with whom he disagreed.

When Richard Nixon ran for president in 1968, Ford supported him. Nixon won that election, and the one in 1972 as well. During President Nixon's second **term,** Vice President Spiro Agnew resigned from office after being accused of tax evasion, not paying money he owed to the government. Nixon had to choose a new vice president. Ford, the honest, well-liked congressman from Michigan, seemed to be a good choice. The FBI ran its most thorough investigation in history on Gerald Ford. He passed the test and was approved quickly.

Ford was sworn into office as the new vice president on December 6, 1973.

All was not well, however. President Nixon faced another, more serious problem: the Watergate **scandal.** Before the election of 1972, Nixon's supporters had broken into the Democratic Party's offices at the Watergate Hotel in Washington, D.C. They went there to steal information to help Nixon beat the Democratic candidate in the election. The burglars were caught, and members of Nixon's staff went to jail.

Representative Ford (left) supported his friend Richard Nixon (right) in two presidential elections.

All along, Nixon claimed that he had played no part in these illegal activities. But more and more evidence appeared. It looked as though Nixon was guilty. Congress prepared to **impeach** the president. Before that could happen, Nixon became the first president to resign from office.

On August 9, 1974, eight months after he became vice president, Gerald Ford became president of the United States. At his **inauguration,** Ford said, "I assume the presidency under extraordinary circumstances…. This is an hour of history that troubles our minds and hurts our hearts." He knew his task would be to heal a nation hurt by a president's dishonesty, and it would not be easy.

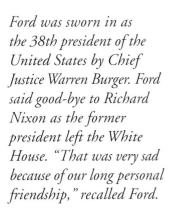

Ford was sworn in as the 38th president of the United States by Chief Justice Warren Burger. Ford said good-bye to Richard Nixon as the former president left the White House. "That was very sad because of our long personal friendship," recalled Ford.

IN AUGUST OF 1947, FRIENDS introduced Ford to Betty Bloomer Warren. She was a former model and dancer who worked as a fashion coordinator at a large department store. Ford liked Betty's energy and honesty. But although he admired her, he had little time for dating. He was determined to have a career in politics. Ford later said that when he met Betty, he "had no idea that someone special had just come into my life." Betty felt the same way. She liked Ford but also led a busy life. They saw each other occasionally, but both agreed not to take their friendship too seriously.

That Christmas, Ford traveled to Idaho for a ski vacation, and Betty attended fashion shows in New York City. The separation made them realize how much they missed each other. The following February, Ford proposed. "I'd like to marry you," was how he put it, "but we can't get married until next fall." He had promised to keep his campaign for Congress a secret and could not even tell his future wife. Finally, his plans became public, and Betty even helped with the campaign. On October 15th, less than a month before the election, Ford and Betty were married. In this photograph, the happy couple walks out of Grace Episcopal Church in Grand Rapids following the wedding ceremony.

Chapter FOUR

The Presidency

President Ford entered office on August 9, 1974. His would be a short presidency—less than two and a half years. But Ford had never hoped to become president. "I look back and wonder how it ever happened to me," he once said.

ONE MONTH AFTER FORD BECAME PRESIDENT, he was forced to make one of the most difficult decisions of his life. He wanted to help the country recover from the Watergate scandal. To do so, he decided to pardon Richard Nixon of all criminal charges. This meant that Nixon would not be punished for his dishonest actions.

Some people claimed that Ford had made a deal with the former president. After all, the two men had been friends for many years. But this was not the case. Ford simply believed that pardoning Nixon was the best way for the nation to move on and forget Watergate. He believed he was doing the best thing for the country by ending the matter quickly. Some people agreed, but many did not. "I have to say that most of my staff

disagreed with me over the pardon," Ford said later. "But I was absolutely convinced that it was the right thing to do."

President Ford faced many other problems as well. He had little experience dealing with foreign affairs, the nation's dealings with other countries. **Inflation** was a serious problem as well. Prices were high on everything from food to housing. Many Americans were out of work. Gas and oil supplies were dwindling. Ford had entered office at a very difficult time.

President Ford announced his pardon of Richard Nixon on September 8, 1974, just one month after he entered office. This act angered many Americans, who felt that Nixon should be punished for what he had done.

Interesting Facts

▶ President Ford selected the former governor of New York, Nelson A. Rockefeller, to be his vice president in 1974. He selected Robert Dole as his running mate in the election of 1976.

▶ Ford still considered Richard Nixon a friend after the Watergate scandal. "Nixon was a long-time friend who made a very stupid mistake," Ford once said. "Everyone is human and can make mistakes."

In addition, Congress was made up mostly of Democrats. They were against most of Ford's ideas because he was a Republican. He had to find ways to **compromise** on some issues. The ability to compromise allowed Ford to solve some problems in the United States. Inflation decreased, and more than four million unemployed Americans found jobs during his presidency. Ford also worked to improve relations with other nations. He made goodwill trips to many foreign countries, including Japan, China, and several European nations. He

President and Mrs. Ford were a good team. Americans liked the friendly and open first lady. During the campaign of 1976, people wore buttons that read, "Keep Betty in the White House" and "Elect Betty's Husband." "I think we're going to have to run Betty for president," Jerry Ford joked.

hosted foreign leaders who came to observe the nation's bicentennial (its 200th birthday) in 1976. Henry Kissinger was Ford's secretary of state, which means that he was in charge of the nation's dealings with other countries. Kissinger worked to build and keep good relations with other nations.

Ford had to deal with another serious problem in May of 1975. In Asia, Cambodian gunboats seized an American merchant ship, the *Mayaguez*. Ford quickly ordered U.S. forces to retake the ship. The *Mayaguez* and 39 crewmen were saved.

The next presidential election took place in 1976. Ford barely won the Republican nomination for president over Ronald Reagan of California. Ford and the vice presidential candidate, Robert Dole, ran against the Democratic candidate, Jimmy Carter. Ford lost to Carter in one of the closest presidential races in history. On January 20, 1977, President Carter graciously began his inauguration speech by praising President Ford: "For myself and for our nation, I want to thank my **predecessor** [President Ford] for all he has done to heal our land."

President and Mrs. Ford retired to their new home in Rancho Mirage, California. He wrote his memoirs in a book called *A Time to Heal: The Autobiography of Gerald R. Ford*. It was published in 1979. In 1981, the Gerald R. Ford Library in Ann Arbor and the Gerald R. Ford Museum in Grand Rapids opened to honor the former president. Since that time, Ford has toured the country giving speeches about politics and current issues. He has also written another book called *Humor and the Presidency*.

In 1976, President Ford barely won the Republican nomination for president. Another candidate, Ronald Reagan (shown to the left of Ford), came in a close second. Reagan was elected president four years later, in 1980.

Ford has remained active in the Republican Party. He travels around the country to campaign for its candidates. He also speaks at universities, informing students about how the U.S. government works.

President Ford has been the recipient of many awards. In August of 1999, President Bill Clinton presented him with the Presidential Medal of Freedom, the highest award presented to U.S. citizens. It honored Gerald Ford for his role in the peaceful handling of the Watergate scandal and of Nixon's resignation. Two months later, in October of 1999, President and Mrs. Ford received the highest honor awarded by the U.S. Congress, the Congressional Gold Medal.

Gerald Ford was president for only about two and a half years, but during that time, he was able to restore Americans' faith in the nation's most important position. This may have been Ford's most significant accomplishment. When asked how he hoped his brief time in office would be remembered, the former president replied, "I hope historians will write that the Ford **administration** healed the land, that I restored public confidence in the White House and in government."

AS FIRST LADY, BETTY FORD BELIEVED HER ROLE WAS TO "SEE AS MANY people as possible and tell them about the integrity, leadership, and honesty of the president." But she is also remembered for her support of the equal rights **amendment** (ERA). This proposed amendment to the **Constitution** promised equal rights to all women in the United States.

Mrs. Ford believed women should have the same chances as men to get a good education, have a fulfilling career, or pursue other opportunities. She traveled around the country giving speeches and interviews about ERA. She wrote letters to congressmen urging them to pass it. Mrs. Ford also encouraged her husband to name women to important positions in the government. She believed that all women, whether devoted to motherhood or to a career outside the home, deserved equal rights and opportunities. Even her hard work didn't help make the ERA become law, however. It was never approved by enough states to become part of the Constitution.

Although Mrs. Ford was a hardworking first lady, she had many health problems. Years before, a pinched nerve ended her promising career as a dancer. Later, this problem became more serious, causing a great deal of pain. Then, in 1974, she underwent surgery for breast cancer. Mrs. Ford spoke publicly about her illness. She hoped this would help other women who suffered with the same disease. But through this difficult experience, Mrs. Ford was in terrible pain. To relieve it, she took medication and drank alcohol. Her use of these substances became an **addiction.**

In 1978, the Ford family confronted Betty about her addiction to alcohol and drugs. In April of that year, she agreed to seek treatment for her problem and entered a program at Long Beach Naval Hospital. This program—and her own determination—helped Mrs. Ford overcome addiction. After her recovery, she spoke openly about her problem. She believed that her willingness to discuss it might encourage others with similar problems to get help. In 1987, a television movie was made about her life. That same year, she published a book, *Betty: A Glad Awakening.* Both told of Mrs. Ford's successful treatment.

In 1982, Mrs. Ford helped establish the Betty Ford Center in Rancho Mirage, California. This facility was founded to help people who suffer from alcohol and drug addiction. Today it is considered one of the best treatment centers in the world. It has helped nearly 40,000 people overcome addiction. Mrs. Ford continues to speak out about alcoholism and drug abuse. "As a recovering alcoholic woman," she says, "I know first hand how the disease of alcoholism and other drug addiction can affect the lives of families and loved ones. Sadly, there is still very little assistance available for anyone whose life has been touched by this disease." She hopes the Betty Ford Center will help to change this.

1913 Gerald R. Ford Jr. is born on July 14. His birth name is Leslie Lynch King Jr.

1916 On February 1, Ford's mother, Dorothy, marries Gerald R. Ford Sr.

1927 At age 14, Ford achieves the rank of Eagle Scout and tries out for the high school football team.

1931 Ford enrolls at the University of Michigan at Ann Arbor.

1935 Ford graduates from the University of Michigan. On December 3, Leslie Lynch King Jr. legally changes his name to Gerald Rudolph Ford Jr.

1938 Yale University accepts Ford into its law school.

1941 Ford graduates from Yale University Law School in the upper 25 percent of his class. On December 7, Japan bombs the U.S. naval base at Pearl Harbor in Hawaii. The United States enters World War II.

1942 Ford joins the U.S. Navy in April. His first assignment is as an athletic training officer, and his job is to keep the sailors in shape.

1943 Ford is assigned to an aircraft carrier, the USS *Monterey.* He is a gunnery officer and is also in charge of physical training for the ship's crew.

1944 In December, Ford nearly loses his life when the *Monterey* is caught in "The Great Typhoon."

1946 Ford is discharged from the navy.

1947 In August, Ford meets his future wife, Betty Bloomer Warren.

1948 On October 15, Gerald Ford and Betty Bloomer Warren are married. Ford is elected to the U.S. House of Representatives in November. He is reelected to the House for 12 more terms.

1951 Ford becomes a member of the House Appropriations Committee in the House of Representatives.

1961 Ford becomes a member of the Defense Appropriations Subcommittee in the House of Representatives.

1963 President John F. Kennedy is assassinated in November. Lyndon Johnson becomes president. Johnson names Ford to the Warren Commission, the group charged with investigating the assassination of President John F. Kennedy.

1965 Ford and John R. Stiles write a book, *Portrait of the Assassin.* Ford is elected the House minority leader.

1968 Ford supports Richard Nixon in the presidential election. Nixon is elected the 37th president of the United States.

1972 Nixon is reelected president.

1973 Nixon chooses Ford as his vice president after Spiro T. Agnew resigns.

1974 On August 9, President Richard Nixon resigns. Ford is sworn in as the 38th president of the United States. On August 20, President Ford selects former governor of New York Nelson A. Rockefeller to be the vice president. On September 8, President Ford pardons Nixon, which means that Nixon will not be punished for his involvement in the Watergate scandal. This act angers many Americans. On November 17, President Ford departs for a visit to Japan. It is the first visit by a U.S. President to that country. He also visits South Korea and the Soviet Union.

1975 On May 12, Cambodia seizes a U.S. merchant ship, the *Mayaguez.* President Ford orders military action, and the ship and crew are rescued. On July 19, President Ford formally announces his candidacy for election in 1976.

1976 The Republican Party nominates Ford as their candidate. On November 2, President Ford loses the presidential election. Jimmy Carter is elected the 39th president.

1979 President Ford publishes his memoirs, *A Time to Heal: The Autobiography of Gerald R. Ford.*

1987 Ford writes another book, *Humor and the Presidency.*

1999 In August, President Clinton presents Gerald Ford with the Presidential Medal of Freedom. In October, President and Mrs. Ford receive the Congressional Gold Medal, the highest award given by Congress.

2000 In July, Ford suffers a stroke while attending the Republican Party National Convention. He is hospitalized but recovers in one week.

addiction (uh-DIK-shun)
An addiction is a habit that a person cannot give up. Betty Ford suffered an addiction to alcohol and drugs.

**administration
(ad-min-ih-STRAY-shun)**
An administration is the time during which a person holds office. Ford hoped his administration had restored confidence in the presidency.

amendment (uh-MEND-ment)
An amendment is a change or addition made to the U.S. Constitution. The equal rights amendment promised equal rights to American women.

assassinate (uh-SASS-ih-nayt)
To assassinate means to murder someone, especially a well-known person. Ford was part of a committee that investigated President Kennedy's assassination.

campaign (kam-PAYN)
A campaign is the process of running for an election, including activities such as giving speeches or attending rallies. Ford kept his campaign for the House of Representatives a secret for many months.

candidate (KAN-dih-det)
A candidate is a person running in an election. The Republicans chose Ford as their candidate for Congress in 1948.

compromise (KOM-pruh-myz)
A compromise is a way to settle a disagreement in which both sides give up part of what they want. Ford was able to compromise with his opponents in Congress during his presidency.

constitution (kon-stih-TOO-shun)
A constitution is the set of basic principles that govern a state, country, or society. The equal rights amendment did not become part of the U.S. Constitution.

impeach (im-PEECH)
If the House of Representatives votes to impeach, it charges the president with a crime or serious misdeed. Congress prepared to impeach President Nixon in 1974.

inauguration (ih-nawg-yuh-RAY-shun)
An inauguration is the ceremony that takes place when a new president begins a term. Ford's inauguration took place on August 9, 1974.

inflation (in-FLAY-shun)
Inflation is a sharp and sudden rise in the price of goods. Inflation was a serious problem when Gerald Ford became president.

isolationism (ice-uh-LAY-shun-iz-um)
Isolationism is a country's policy of staying out of the affairs of other countries. The United States had a policy of isolationism before World War II.

navigation (nav-ih-GAY-shun)
Navigation is the science of determining the position and course of a ship, airplane, or other craft. Ford learned about navigation while he worked on the USS *Monterey*.

Nazi Party (NAHT-see PAR-tee)
The Nazi Party was a political party that ruled Germany from 1933 to 1945. The Nazis blamed other countries and races for the problems that Germany faced after World War I.

nomination (nom-ih-NAY-shun)
If someone receives a nomination, he or she is chosen by a political party to run for an office. To run for Congress, Ford had to win the Republican Party nomination.

officer (AW-feh-ser)
An officer is a leader in the military who commands other soldiers. Ford's first assignment in the navy was as an athletic training officer.

**political parties
(puh-LIT-ih-kul PAR-teez)**
Political parties are groups of people who share similar ideas about how to run a government. The Republican Party is one of the nation's two most powerful political parties.

politician (pawl-ih-TISH-un)
A politician is a person who holds an office in government. Ford was a politician.

predecessor (PRED-eh-ses-ur)
A predecessor is someone who holds a position or office before another person. Ford was President Carter's predecessor.

promoted (pruh-MOH-ted)
People who are promoted receive a more important job or position to recognize their good work. While in the navy, Ford was quickly promoted from ensign to lieutenant.

scandal (SKAN-dl)
A scandal is a shameful action that shocks the public. When President Nixon was involved in dishonest activities, it was considered a scandal.

term (TERM)
A term is the length of time a politician can keep his or her position by law. A U.S. president's term is four years.

Our PRESIDENTS

President	Birthplace	Life Dates	Term	Political Party	First Lady
George Washington	Virginia	1732–1799	1789–1797	None	Martha Dandridge Custis Washington
John Adams	Massachusetts	1735–1826	1797–1801	Federalist	Abigail Smith Adams
Thomas Jefferson	Virginia	1743–1826	1801–1809	Democratic-Republican	widower
James Madison	Virginia	1751–1836	1809–1817	Democratic-Republican	Dolley Payne Todd Madison
James Monroe	Virginia	1758–1831	1817–1825	Democratic-Republican	Elizabeth "Eliza" Kortright Monroe
John Quincy Adams	Massachusetts	1767–1848	1825–1829	Democratic-Republican	Louisa Catherine Johnson Adams
Andrew Jackson	South Carolina	1767–1845	1829–1837	Democrat	widower
Martin Van Buren	New York	1782–1862	1837–1841	Democrat	widower
William Henry Harrison	Virginia	1773–1841	1841	Whig	Anna Tuthill Symmes Harrison
John Tyler	Virginia	1790–1862	1841–1845	Whig	Letitia Christian Tyler Julia Gardiner Tyler
James Polk	North Carolina	1795–1849	1845–1849	Democrat	Sarah Childress Polk

Our PRESIDENTS

President	Birthplace	Life Dates	Term	Political Party	First Lady
Zachary Taylor	Virginia	1784–1850	1849–1850	Whig	Margaret Mackall Smith Taylor
Millard Fillmore	New York	1800–1874	1850–1853	Whig	Abigail Powers Fillmore
Franklin Pierce	New Hampshire	1804–1869	1853–1857	Democrat	Jane Means Appleton Pierce
James Buchanan	Pennsylvania	1791–1868	1857–1861	Democrat	never married
Abraham Lincoln	Kentucky	1809–1865	1861–1865	Republican	Mary Todd Lincoln
Andrew Johnson	North Carolina	1808–1875	1865–1869	Democrat	Eliza McCardle Johnson
Ulysses S. Grant	Ohio	1822–1885	1869–1877	Republican	Julia Dent Grant
Rutherford B. Hayes	Ohio	1822–1893	1877–1881	Republican	Lucy Ware Webb Hayes
James A. Garfield	Ohio	1831–1881	1881	Republican	Lucretia Rudolph Garfield
Chester A. Arthur	Vermont	1829–1886	1881–1885	Republican	widower
Grover Cleveland	New Jersey	1837–1908	1885–1889	Democrat	Frances Folsom Cleveland

Our PRESIDENTS

President	Birthplace	Life Dates	Term	Political Party	First Lady
Benjamin Harrison	Ohio	1833–1901	1889–1893	Republican	Caroline Lavina Scott Harrison
Grover Cleveland	New Jersey	1837–1908	1893–1897	Democrat	Frances Folsom Cleveland
William McKinley	Ohio	1843–1901	1897–1901	Republican	Ida Saxton McKinley
Theodore Roosevelt	New York	1858–1919	1901–1909	Republican	Edith Kermit Carow Roosevelt
William Howard Taft	Ohio	1857–1930	1909–1913	Republican	Helen Herron Taft
Woodrow Wilson	Virginia	1856–1924	1913–1921	Democrat	Ellen L. Axson Wilson Edith Bolling Galt Wilson
Warren G. Harding	Ohio	1865–1923	1921–1923	Republican	Florence Kling De Wolfe Harding
Calvin Coolidge	Vermont	1872–1933	1923–1929	Republican	Grace Anna Goodhue Coolidge
Herbert Hoover	Iowa	1874–1964	1929–1933	Republican	Lou Henry Hoover
Franklin D. Roosevelt	New York	1882–1945	1933–1945	Democrat	Anna Eleanor Roosevelt Roosevelt
Harry S. Truman	Missouri	1884–1972	1945–1953	Democrat	Elizabeth "Bess" Virginia Wallace Truman

Our Presidents

President	Birthplace	Life Dates	Term	Political Party	First Lady
Dwight D. Eisenhower	Texas	1890–1969	1953–1961	Republican	Mamie Geneva Doud Eisenhower
John F. Kennedy	Massachusetts	1917–1963	1961–1963	Democrat	Jacqueline Lee Bouvier Kennedy
Lyndon Baines Johnson	Texas	1908–1973	1963–1969	Democrat	Claudia "Lady Bird" Alta Taylor Johnson
Richard M. Nixon	California	1913–1994	1969–1974	Republican	Thelma "Pat" Catherine Patricia Ryan Nixon
Gerald R. Ford	Nebraska	1913–	1974–1977	Republican	Elizabeth "Betty" Bloomer Warren Ford
James Earl Carter	Georgia	1924–	1977–1981	Democrat	Rosalynn Smith Carter
Ronald Reagan	Illinois	1911–	1981–1989	Republican	Nancy Davis Reagan
George Bush	Massachusetts	1924–	1989–1993	Republican	Barbara Pierce Bush
William J. Clinton	Arkansas	1946–	1993–2001	Democrat	Hillary Rodham Clinton
George W. Bush	Connecticut	1946–	2001–	Republican	Laura Welch Bush

Presidential FACTS

Qualifications
To run for president, a candidate must
- be at least 35 years old
- be a citizen who was born in the United States
- have lived in the United States for 14 years

Term of Office
A president's term of office is four years. No president can stay in office for more than two terms.

Election Date
The presidential election takes place every four years on the first Tuesday of November.

Inauguration Date
Presidents are inaugurated on January 20.

Oath of Office
I do solemnly swear I will faithfully execute the office of the President of the United States and will to the best of my ability preserve, protect, and defend the Constitution of the United States.

Write a Letter to the President
One of the best things about being a U.S. citizen is that Americans get to participate in their government. They can speak out if they feel government leaders aren't doing their jobs. They can also praise leaders who are going the extra mile. Do you have something you'd like the president to do? Should the president worry more about the environment and encourage people to recycle? Should the government spend more money on our schools? You can write a letter to the president to say how you feel!

1600 Pennsylvania Avenue
Washington, D.C. 20500

You can even send an c-mail to: president@whitehouse.gov

For Further INFORMATION

Internet Sites

Visit the Gerald Ford Library:
http://www.ford.utexas.edu/

Read Ford's speech pardoning President Richard Nixon:
http://www.historyplace.com/speeches/ford.htm

Read an essay about Gerald Ford:
http://www.pbs.org/newshour/character/essays/ford.html

Learn more about Richard Nixon and the Watergate scandal:
http://www.nixonfoundation.org/

Learn more about all the presidents and visit the White House:
http://www.whitehouse.gov/WH/glimpse/presidents/html/presidents.html
http://www.thepresidency.org/presinfo.htm
http://www.americanpresidents.org/

Books

Cohen, Daniel. *Watergate: Deception in the White House* (Spotlight on American History). Brookfield, CT: Millbrook Press, 1998.

Gaines, Ann Graham. *Richard M. Nixon: Our Thirty-Seventh President.* Chanhassen, MN: The Child's World, Inc., 2002.

Sipiera, Paul P. *Gerald Ford: Thirty-Eighth President of the United States* (Encyclopedia of Presidents). Chicago: Childrens Press, 1989.

Index

Agnew, Spiro T., 26, 39
Amberg, Julius, 22
Atwood, Pappy, 16-19

Betty Ford Center, 37
bicentennial, 33, 37
Buchen, Philip A., 13
Bush, George W., 35

Cambodia, 33, 39
Carter, Jimmy, 33, 39
civil rights, 37
Clinton, Bill, 35
Congressional Gold Medal, 35, 39

Defense Appropriations Subcommittee, 25, 38
Democratic Party, 27, 32
discrimination, 37
Dole, Robert, 32-33

equal rights, 36

Ford, Betty, 24, 29, 32, 34-35, 36-37, 38-39
Ford, Dorothy, 6-8, 25, 38
Ford, Gerald R., Jr.
    athleticism of, 8-12, 38
    awards for, 35, 39
    birth of, 7, 38
    books by, 26, 35, 38-39
    campaign for U.S. Representative, 23-24
    as chairman of Republican National Convention, 26, 39
    civil rights initiatives, 37
    education of, 8-11, 38
    goodwill trips of, 33, 39
    as House minority leader, 26, 38
    law career, 13, 22
    law degree, 11-12, 38
    marriage of, 29, 38
    naval career, 14-20, 38
    pardon of Nixon, 30-31, 39
    as president, 6-7, 30, 34, 36
    retirement of, 34-35
    swearing in as president, 28, 39
    as U.S. Representative, 24-26, 38
    as vice president, 26-28, 39
Ford, Gerald R., Sr., 8, 25, 38

Gerald R. Ford Library, 34
Gerald R. Ford Museum, 34
Great Depression, 9-10
Great Pacific Typhoon, 17-18, 38

Hitler, Adolf, 21
House Appropriations Committee, 25, 38
Humor and the Presidency (Ford), 34, 39

inflation, 31
isolationism, 21

Johnson, Lyndon, 26, 38
Jonkman, Bartel J., 23

Kennedy, John F., 26, 38
King, Dorothy Gardner. See Ford, Dorothy
King, Leslie Lynch, 7-8
King, Leslie Lynch, Jr., 7. See also Ford, Gerald R., Jr.
Kissinger, Henry, 33

Mayaguez, capture of, 33, 39

Nazi Party, 21
Nixon, Richard, 6-7, 24, 26-28, 30, 32, 35, 39

Pearl Harbor, 13, 16, 21, 38
Portrait of the Assassin (Ford and Stiles), 26, 39
Presidential Medal of Freedom, 35, 39

Reagan, Ronald, 33-34
Republican National Convention, 39
Republican Party, 13, 23-24, 32, 35-36
Rockefeller, Nelson A, 32, 39

Stiles, John, 23-24, 39

A Time to Heal: The Autobiography of Gerald R. Ford, 34, 39
unemployment, 32
USS Monterey, 14-20, 38

Walling, Truman, 19
Warren, Betty Bloomer. See Ford, Betty
Warren Commission, 26, 38
Watergate scandal, 27-28, 30-32, 35, 39
World War II, 13, 15-21, 38

Yale University, 11-13, 38